The

Mobile

Marketing

Opportunity

What Every Small Business Owner Needs to Know About Mobile Marketing

By

Loren Squires

HK Marketing Solutions
Denver Colorado
www.Mobile-Marketing-Colorado.com

Income Disclaimer

This document contains business strategies, marketing methods and other business advice that, regardless of my own results and experience, may not produce the same results (or any results) for you. I make absolutely no guarantee, expressed or implied, that by following the advice below you will make any money or improve current profits, as there are several factors and variables that come into play regarding any given business.

Primarily, results will depend on the nature of the product or business model, the conditions of the marketplace, the experience of the individual, and situations and elements that are beyond your control.

As with any business endeavor, you assume all risk related to investment and money based on your own discretion and at your own potential expense.

Liability Disclaimer

By reading this document, you assume all risks associated with using the advice given below, with a full understanding that you, solely, are responsible for anything that may occur as a result of putting this information into action in any way, and regardless of your interpretation of the ad-vice.

You further agree that our company cannot be held responsible in any way for the success or failure of your business as a result of the inform-ation presented below. It is your responsibility to conduct your own due diligence regarding the safe and successful operation of your business if you intend to apply any of our information in any way to your business operations.

Terms of Use

You are given a non-transferable, "personal use" license to this product. You cannot distribute it or share it with other individuals.

Also, there are no resale rights or private label rights granted when purchasing this document. In other words, it's for your own personal use only.

The

Mobile

Marketing

Opportunity

What Every Small Business Owner Needs to Know About Mobile Marketing

Table of Contents

Mobile Marketing

Introduction

More than ever before, small business owners today are faced with a myriad of new and exciting electronic products, systems, and strategies available to them that they can use to increase their business' online exposure. From Facebook to Twitter to video marketing, the list is long and often confusing to the average small business owner.

So as an entrepreneur, you may be asking yourself what is the best, fastest, and most cost-effective way to reach the people in your local marketplace? What is the best online strategy that you can use to generate foot traffic in your place of business, create new customers, and stay connected with your existing clientele?

Even in this dynamic environment, some technologies outshine others. And today nothing represents a bigger "bang" for your advertising buck than mobile marketing. That's because mobile marketing gives small businesses the ability to reach out and find their potential customers instantly -- whenever and wherever they may be.

So why is Mobile Marketing the #1 choice of many savvy business owners all over the world… and in your hometown?

Well let's have a closer look at some facts:

1. With today's smartphones, consumers are accessing the Internet all the time; from work, from sporting events and while watching TV at home. The amount of data flowing across the airwaves is astounding and it's growing at an astonishing rate. Simply put, if your business is not utilizing mobile techniques then you are missing out on potential business.

2. Around the globe today there are roughly 5 BILLION consumers already walking around with a mobile device every day…and that makes contacting these potential customers relatively easy.

3. Most people keep their mobile device within arm's reach 24/7. What does that mean? The use of SMS Text Message Marketing will result in most of your messages being seen and read by the mobile device owner within minutes of being sent. This of course will re-turn higher redemption rates, and bring the possibility of more sales, which in turn leads to more profits.

4. The average American is already spending al-most three hours per day surfing the Internet from their mobile devices. These millions of people represent online traffic that is ready to hear your message.

5. By 2013, the use of mobile Internet usage is expected to surpass traditional desktop Inter-net usage. So the use of mobile marketing technology will be critical if you want to stay ahead of your completion.

6. According to Google, over 50% of searches that use a geographic modifier, (Denver Steak

House, Mexican Restaurant Denver), are performed on a smart phone.

7. 79% of smartphone owners use it to help with shopping

8. 95% look for local information.

9. Of those 95% looking for local information:

> 88% take action within the same day.

> 61% call a business.

> 59% visit a business.

The above facts indicate that if you are not currently leveraging mobile marketing to promote your business, you may soon be left behind by the fast-movers and early adopters of this powerful technology.

Mobile Marketing Options – At a Glance

Here we will cover the three major areas of mobile marketing. Pointing out their current use, trends, projections, and benefits.

Mobile Website Facts and Benefits

• Studies show that current mobile web-user experiences are overall horrible when it comes to viewing and navigating websites. Websites that have not been optimized for mobile viewing are too cluttered and negatively impact the visitor's ability to locate the information they are looking for.

• Traditional websites are designed to be viewed on a computer screen instead of a mobile device. This means that most regular websites are not compatible with mobile devices.

• More and more people are using their mobile devices to access the Internet while on the go.

13

In fact, one-third of the world's population uses their mobile devices to perform Internet searches.

• One-half of all Internet searches for LOCAL products and services are performed on mobile devices.

• Mobile-friendly websites have higher loading speed, making the visitor experience more pleasurable.

• A mobile site helps you attract both "new" and "repeat" customers by giving your business "instant mobile marketability" when your visitors lands on your clean mobile site with all of the important information clearly and easily accessible.

• Can be viewed anytime and anywhere mobile cell phone coverage is available. Due to the massive amount of Internet-enabled mobile devices across the world, this means your website can easily be exposed to millions of people.

• Makes it easier for "On the go" visitors to easily find your business and contact you with one-click calling, one-click email, and instant directions. This eliminates the need for your customers to take "extra steps" in order to contact or visit your business.

• When users are successful in finding what they need while visiting a mobile website, they're more likely to come back. When mobile users land on a website that is hard to navigate and difficult to find the information they're looking for, they quickly exit and make a mental note never to return.

• Mobile sites have the advantage of coming up higher in search engine results for local searches performed on mobile devices. This means that when people search for your product or service using their mobile device, you can show up higher in the results just because you have a mobile website.

• Mobile sites also cause their related desktop versions to rank higher in the search results. Google has stated that websites with a related mobile version will rank higher than others without a mobile site.

• Gives you the advantage over your competitors; most of which are not leveraging the powerful benefits of mobile marketing.

• It is easy to track your mobile success with free reporting and analytic tools available with most mobile platforms. Simply track your visitors and make improvements where necessary.

• Integrating social media platforms such as Facebook, Twitter, and YouTube with your mobile website is simple and will help boost your profits even more.

SMS Text Marketing Facts and Benefits

• According to researchers, 73% of consumers would like to receive special offers on their mobile devices – but they are not getting them.

• Offers made via SMS text marketing have consistently gotten response rates up to 20% - that is 10 times more than traditional advertising methods such as email, direct mail, and newspaper ads which usually get around a 2%-3% response rate.

• Most consumers always have their mobile phone by their side, which means that they will receive your message no matter where they are.

• Studies show that over 90% of consumers read their mobile text messages within minutes.

• Research shows that 29% of mobile users are open to scanning a mobile tag or QR code to get coupons.

• Studies show that mobile coupons will be-come more relevant over the next several years.

• Using QR codes is the perfect way to make it quick and convenient for your audience to opt-in to your SMS list.

• SMS text marketing is a "permission-based" form of marketing where the customer initiates things by texting in a keyword to join your list. In exchange for their subscription, you can of-fer them an incentive, such as a coupon, free goods, free information, etc. Once the person has subscribed to your text messaging list, they are now a member of your list and will re-ceive all of your future text messages.

• SMS text marketing puts your subscribers at ease because they can opt-out of your list at any time. However, since they opted-in to join your list, they usually WANT to receive your messages.

• SMS text messages can go viral, which means they can spread like wildfire. This is because your subscribers will often forward your offers to friends and family, which will give you more exposure and more sales.

• SMS text marketing allows you to reduce your advertising costs while increasing sales and customer loyalty at the same time. This method is inexpensive compared to other marketing methods and usually gets a much higher response rate.

• With SMS text marketing, you can reach a group of people who are interested in knowing about your products and services within minutes.

• SMS text marketing is great for local retailers of all types wishing to promote products or services, provide purchase incentives, and increase customer loyalty, retention, and long-term customer value.

• It's easy to track results of a SMS text marketing campaign as recipients of your text offers usually have to come into your establishment and show you the offer or coupon right on their cell phones in order to redeem it.

• Since most mobile phone users have their phones within reach at all times, SMS text marketing is the ideal way to alert people to time-sensitive information, such as an appointment reminder, or a short-term coupon offer.

QR Codes Facts and Benefits

• QR (Quick Response) codes are 2 dimensional bar codes that are used to transfer information through mobile phone barcode readers.

• Many major companies are using QR codes to brand and advertise such as Walmart, OnStar, Best Buy, Starbucks, Ralph Lauren, Pepsi, and many others.

• QR codes are very affordable to create, they store a lot of data, and they do not require expensive barcode scanning devices to work.

• A QR code scanner is very easy to download, but most mobile smartphones now already come with a QR code scanner installed.

• QR codes are becoming popular with consumers. From January 2010 through December 2010, the number of people who scanned QR codes worldwide shot up by 13 times.

• QR codes are helping businesses generate more leads, more sales, and more long-term customers.

• QR codes simplify the consumer experience by making it possible to "scan" instead of "type" to access your information on their mobile device.

• With the snap of a QR code scanner-equipped smartphone consumers can scan your QR code and INSTANTLY connect to various forms of digital media or retrieve desired information. A QR code can take them to an opt-in form, a website (preferably a mobile-friendly website), directions to an establishment, a coupon, a video, a menu, picture, a

Facebook Fanpage, Twitter page – the possibilities are nearly endless.

• QR codes can help you build a customer list fast. Create a QR code that links to an opt-in page where consumers will leave their name and email address in exchange for some type of incentive.

• QR codes can be easily placed on all of your marketing materials including business cards, T-shirts, flyers, receipts, print advertising, signs, billboards, your website, store windows/displays, and many others.

• QR codes can be linked to your Social Media profiles such as Facebook, Twitter, and YouTube to create a powerful list-building combination.

• You can create QR codes to help you get an increase of customer reviews on all of your online directory listings; such as your Google Places Business Listing, Yelp, Insider Reviews, Super Pages, etc. Good online customer reviews are powerful in converting your prospects into new customers.

• Traditional advertising methods require printing and publishing, which can cost thousands. But there are no printing costs involved with

QR codes. And it's easy to make changes to your destination when things change – you don't have to worry about changing your ad and then re-printing and re-publishing. And there are some QR code providers that allow your to change the destination of the QR code.

Does Mobile Marketing Fit Well With Your Business?

There are many factors that you should consider before jumping into mobile marketing for you own business. Even if you have enough money to invest, understand all of the privacy issues involved in mobile marketing, and think that you're pretty much good to go, you should first consider the type of business that you own, and your specific promotional needs.

The Kind of Business You Run Matters

What kind of business are you in? Are you an online retailer, or an offline brick and mortar company or both? Are you a services provider or a product merchant? Are your goods tangible, such as shoes, clothes, books, food, or drink? Or are your goods "virtual" in nature, such as ebooks, software, or online subscriptions?

23

Offline businesses can benefit greatly by using mobile marketing. For instance, restaurants, retailers, automotive repair shops, beauty salons, realtors, chiropractors, dentists, etc. can all use mobile marketing very effectively to promote their business. Do you have a special offer, a coupon, or a discount that would apply to your business? Chances are your customers will be very receptive to receiving messages from you to let them know this is the case.

Businesses who cater to an older demographic may not do so well with mobile marketing. Although mobile phones are very popular with young and old alike, the truth is that the older generation above 60 years of age still is not very comfortable with the current cell phone technology.

Many of these people are likely using older model cell phones that are not smartphones and may not be able to pull up mobile-ready websites. Some of the older models being used today don't even have internet access.

Even those that do have access to the Internet on their cell phones may not be comfortable enough with the technology to respond to your marketing messages.

For example, businesses such as diabetic supply companies, denture manufacturers, and any services and products geared towards the 50-plus market may want to seriously consider if mobile marketing is going to be worth the time and money. It does not mean that the older generation does not use cell phones or the Internet. It simply means that there are more challenges with this market in terms of mobile marketing methods.

Another point to keep in mind is the action that you want your target market to consider after receiving your mobile marketing messages. Do you want them to come to the store and buy something? Do you want them to buy online? Do you want them to call?

Because the cell phone is a very personal item to your audience, you really want to be sure that you have an appropriate marketing funnel in place. In addition, you want to be sure that you have tracking and measuring features in place. This enables you to understand the mobile marketing phenomenon closer and helps to avoid costly mistakes in the future.

"But My Website Appears on a Mobile Device"

If my website appears on a mobile device isn't that mobile enough?

In a word, NO. That is, if you'd like to turn that website visitor into a customer.

Your standard desktop/laptop website may appear on a smart phone, (if it isn't made with 'Flash'), but its lack of usefulness will quickly make that visitor look elsewhere for the information, goods, or services they are seeking.

If smart phone visitors are faced with constant scrolling up and down, and sideways, and constant zooming in and out just to read your website, then you are NOT providing them with any help to learn more about you, and to reach a buying decision about what you have to offer.

Although desktop/laptop websites, and mobile-friendly websites use the same internet, there are major differences in what people are looking for. There are also technological, aesthetic, and purposes that make them quite different in how you should attack the issue of turning visitors into customers.

Different Devices Have Different Capabilities

Just like the smart phone or tablet is considered a device, the desktop or laptop computer should also be considered a device. And as such they have their own technologies that give them their own set of capabilities.

Mobile devices, be it smart phones or tablets, also have their own technologies which give them their own set of abilities and limitations. A mobile device can actually do things a desktop/laptop cannot, and of course, vice versa.

It is not the internet that is different, it is the device and associated technologies that are different. As such, the two different means of accessing the internet demand two different methods of information presentation.

The most obvious examples are the size of the screen, and also the method of connecting to the internet.

For example, on a desktop or laptop site you can include multiple videos, large images, and Flash animation, but that won't work on mobile due to access methods, browser limitations, and screen size.

However, mobile has its own unique functionalities. For example, your mobile device can pinpoint your location within a few feet thanks to GPS, something missing from desktop and laptop computers. Additionally, smart phones have features that aren't available on desktops/laptops, such as being able to tap on a phone number from a website to be instantly connected.

Mobile websites need to adapt to different design and layout constraints.

Because desktop/laptop websites have been around for so long, we've gotten used to the standard layout and design that has evolved over time. We know what to expect when it comes to navigation and content possibilities.

But mobile is a whole new frontier. And as such, requires a new layout and content formatting in order to get your message across to those accessing your website on a smart phone.

For example, because of screen size, menus need to take up as little space a possible. But at the same time, provide the visitor with intuitive navigation.

Vast quantities of text don't work either. Brevity needs to be the order of the day. Say what needs to be said in as little space as possible. Having less text that is larger and easier to read creates more comfort to the visitor, and makes it much more likely that your content will actually be read at all. Zooming in and out just to read your content is a nice feature, but it's a major turn-off that will drive your potential customers to another website that is easier to read.

Even photos and images can be too small to communicate with. Don't make your website visitors work just to be communicated with. They won't stand for that, and will quickly leave, not to return.

Good Mobile Sites Maintain a Single Focus

Keep it simple, make it easy to use, keep it brief, and to the point.

People searching on their smart phones use the internet differently that those searching on a desktop or laptop computer. They usually already know what they are looking for, and just need to know where it is located, what you offer, and what it costs.

Thanks to increasingly larger monitors and faster Internet connections, traditional websites have grown to include dozens of sections with a lot of content. A quick look at the Yahoo! homepage demonstrates just how much content can be on a single page.

Mobile devices, however because of their limited screen size, have a limited viewing area, which means it's important for each mobile page to have a single focus. That is, turning a visitor into a customer.

A mobile website needs to be simple, to the point, easy to view, and have intuitive navigation. For example, since most mobile users already know what they are looking for, your site needs to give that to them. Your location, a map of where you are, and your hours of operation need to be prominent. Your offering of goods and/or services need to be easy to ascertain. And it must be easy to read on a much smaller screen that if they were to find you on a desktop or laptop computer.

Each page needs to be focused on a single idea, or a hierarchy of your goods and/or services. And then, finally through intuitive navigation, the actual product or service you are offering.

If you can differentiate your mobile site from your standard desktop/laptop website, and give your different visitors what they are looking for, then your mobile website will quickly become a customer magnet, with its effects directly impacting your bottom line. And isn't that why you have a website in the first place?

Why Your Business Needs a 'Mobile- Friendly' Website

So how to you implement this strategy in your own business to increase your sales and connect with new customers? Choosing the right strategy to reach current and future customers is the key to your success.

For example, simply "mobilizing" your company's existing website does not mean you are open for business. Unless your website or blog is mobile optimized for different cell phones and devices, it will not fit the screen properly. For example, mobile devices are too small to view standard web-based content, which means the end user must scroll up and down, from side to side, and zoom in and out in order to find the relevant information about your company's products and services.

In fact, if your site is not optimized for mobile devices it may not download or be viewable at all on a cell phone screen. If the site is not easy to navigate, a potential customer will quickly exit and move on to another site, possibly a local competitor.

And with literally millions of people searching for information on mobile devices every day, it's apparent that if your company's website is not mobile-optimized, you could be losing out on a lot of business.

Let's have a closer look at a few reasons why your business should have a mobile website.

A key to the enormous growth of mobile phones in the past several years is the fact that they are so handy and portable, and can be taken with you anywhere. In fact, most people have their mobile phone within arm's reach 24 hours a day.

Why? Well because of the portability and robust search capabilities of today's devices, they have to a large extent replaced traditional laptops or desktop computers. As a result, you will see people using mobile devices at work, shopping, sporting events and while stuck in traffic. Therefore, to maintain the proper mobile presence with today's consumers, a mobile optimized website is essential.

Today's smart phones come preloaded with search engines, allowing access to Google and Yahoo, giving your business the possibility of be- ing "found" on page one of these search engines for local search results related to your business and location, (with proper SEO – Search Engine Optimization of course). Of course, if your site does not render properly because it is not mobile optimized, this ability for consumers to connect with you via these search engines will often do you no good, resulting in the loss of a potential new customer.

Having a "mobile-friendly" website for your com- pany simply means that new customers will be able to find you from wherever they are search- ing. You will be able to meet them wherever and whenever they are online, and they will be able to obtain the information that they are searching for since your company's website is formatted properly to their mobile device.

This will go a long way to providing your mobile website visitors with a welcoming and useful experience, and is more likely to turn them from visitors into customers.

Here's a brief graphic of how having a separate mobile website works.

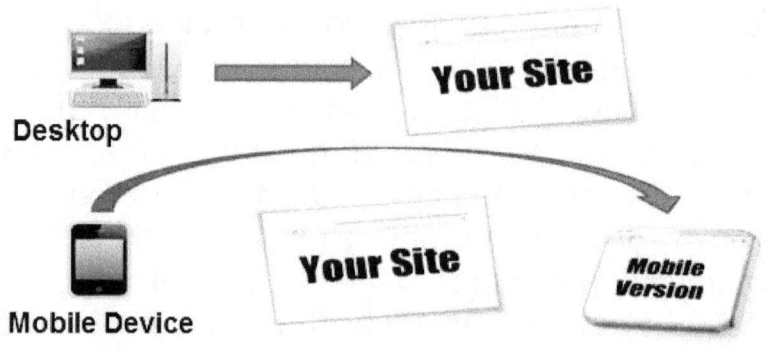

When a smartphone user visits your website, it will immediately sense that, and automatically redirect the visitor to the separate mobile website. All without them knowing what happened. They are simply presented with the much more mobile-friendly and easier to use mobile site.

Elements of Good Mobile Website Design

Simplicity is King

If you really want to impress your mobile website visitors and provide them with an experience that will make them more likely to buy from you, then these three ideas are critical in the design of the mobile site – ease of use, functionality, and simplicity.

The website needs to be easy to use. The screen is tiny, most fingers are not. Icons and buttons need to be large enough to be easily operated.

The website needs to function in a very uncomplicated manner. There's not much space there to tell people how to navigate and get around in your site. It needs to be intuitive.

The website needs to be simple. Notice that doesn't mean void of content. It means to present your content as simply as possible. Bells and whistles only serve to complicate things, slow down page loading, and create difficulties for your visitors.

The manner in which people use a mobile website is significantly different than how they use a website on a desktop or laptop.

Think of it this way - a desktop or laptop website is designed for people who are looking for information, education, sales data, and a host of other information that can be gleaned from the website. Whereas a mobile website is for people who basically already know what they are looking for, and need to find where and how to get it.

For an example, compare Google.com with Yahoo.com. A mobile site should be more Google and a lot less Yahoo.

Color it simply

Not leaving white space on your mobile website is really tough on the eyes of your visitors. The small screen size makes adequate white space an important factor in creating a pleasant browsing experience for your visitors.

Navigation needs to be in clear and in easy-to-see colors. Funky color schemes that look great on a desktop or laptop browser can be confusing and hard on the eyes when viewed on a mobile

device. Good contrast is key in making your mobile content appealing on such a small screen.

The Phone Number Is a Must

If you do not have a phone number prominently
displayed on your mobile website, you have
failed. It's just that simple. It is still surprising to
see the number of regular websites that don't
have the business' phone number displayed in a
manner that's easy to find. Its in small type at
the bottom of the screen, or on the 'contact page'
only. Not a good idea.

And on a smartphone, its got be there in more
than one location. After all, they are viewing your
site on a phone.

Tap to Call

One way to make it really easy for someone to
call you is the 'tap to call' feature. This is where
your logo is made into a clickable link. All the
visitor then has to do is tap the screen on the
logo and a call will be automatically placed to the
phone number of the business. Think of it as like
a menu button, except this button take them directly to the business.

Videos, Images, and Flash

In three words: avoid, minimize, and avoid, re-spectively.

Video greatly slows down the speed in which a site can download onto a mobile phone. And some smartphones don't have the horsepower to run them well without a lot of stopping and start-ing. This is not a good experience for your visit-or.

Images are they same way if they are not scaled down. Use proper graphic software to scale them. The larger they are, the slower they will appear.

Flash is basically a movie or animation. They play fine on the vast majority of desktops and laptops. But there are many smartphones that can not play flash. If your site is built with flash, it will appear as a blank screen on a smartphone that doesn't do flash. And if you have flash videos embedded within your website, those will appear as blank holes on the smartphone screen. This is definitely not conducive to a pleasant user experience.

Use Simple Navigation

Simple navigation is a must on a mobile website. Buttons and clickable icons need to be large enough for easy use. Also burying information under multiple layers of pages is bound to frus-trate your visitors.

Download Speed

Another consideration for the mobile website is how much time it takes to download and appear complete on the visitor's smartphone. Nobody wants to wait around for 1 to 3 minutes while your website is loading.

A mobile website should download and appear complete in just a few seconds. A slow site just frustrates visitors, and gives them incentive to move on to a better designed site. Something you don't want to occur.

Use Valid Markup Code

Mobile browsers are not nearly as forgiving for bad code as desktop browsers. To insure a high level of mobile-friendliness, be sure to validate the HTML and CSS code of your mobile website.

So, when looking to build, or have built, a mobile website remember the three critical criteria for it to be successful – ease of use, functionality, and simplicity.

A Mobile Website or a Mobile App?

There is currently a fair amount of debate about what is the best way to 'go mobile', a mobile website or a mobile app. If you're just now considering going mobile you're probably wondering that yourself. There are different reasons for going one way or the other.

Here we'll discuss many of the different considerations to take into account when making this decision. First, so we're starting on the same foundation, a couple of definitions.

What is a mobile website?

A mobile website is similar to any other website in that it consists of content, and presentation coding. The content is the information you wish to communicate with people when they visit your website. The presentation code is called HTML, computer code that is used by an internet browser to display your content.

It is the same for a mobile website as it is for a desktop/laptop website. The defining difference

43

is the device that your website visitors are using to view your information. And that difference is HUGE.

This is very easy to see. Look at your smart-phone screen. Now look at your desktop/laptop screen. Night and day, yes? And some things that work well during the day, may not work well at night. Size makes most of the difference.

The other difference is that cable. You don't see many people walking around trailing a long coax cable. That is the other difference: the way these devices access the internet. This wireless as-pect of connecting to the internet must be con-sidered when building a mobile website.

With these differences a mobile website must present and behave in a manner dissimilar to the desktop/laptop environment.

What is a mobile app?

A mobile application is essentially software spe-cially developed to run on mobile devices. Apps are actual software applications that are down-loaded, installed, and then reside on a mobile device, rather than being displayed within an in-ternet browser.

These mobile apps generally do more than just display information. They are logical machines that perform functions. Games are the major player in mobile apps, but apps can do other things as well. Such as mapping, voice recording, note taking, emailing, and others. They are more functional than simple presentation of content.

In order for some one to use a mobile app they must first visit an app marketplace, such as the Apple App Store, or the Android Market, or the Blackberry App World.

This points out one of the major hurdles that people face with apps. You must go find it, download it, and then install it. It is not just going someplace on the internet that displays information.

These different app stores point out the other major hurdle, apps are not platform independent. That is, an Apple app won't run on an Android device and vice versa. If you want to build an app, you must build at least two different versions of the same app. This gets costly.

Now that the definitions are out of the way, let's compare how they stack up against each other.

To be sure, there are times when one or the other is superior. A lot depends on your purpose for going mobile. But when it comes to marketing, one stands above the other. Let's take a look.

Mobile Website Advantages over Mobile Apps

If you're considering jumping into the mobile marketing arena, a mobile website is almost always going to make a lot of sense for a practical first step. There are many serious advantages that a mobile website has over a mobile app. Here we will take a look at some of these advantages.

Instant Accessibility

A mobile website is instantly accessible for people to find easily and quickly through a search engine. However, apps need to be found, then downloaded from an app marketplace, then installed before one can make use of them. And that's assuming that people even know you have an app. These extra steps can be a significant hindrance and are not helpful in getting your message out to the public.

Platform Independence

Mobile websites are accessible to all. You don't need one mobile website for Apple products, and another separate website for Android products. If a device can surf the web, then it can view a mobile optimized website.

Whereas, apps on the other hand are platform dependent. To have an app be available to everyone, you would need three separate versions, one for Apple, one for Android, and one for Blackberry.

Additionally, mobile website URLs can be integrated into other marketing avenues. Such as SMS text marketing, and QR codes.

Easy to Upgrade and Enhance

A mobile website is usually much more dynamic and flexible when it comes to updating content, design, and features. Think of a standard website, how easy that is to make changes to. Virtually whenever you want.

An app, on the other hand, is much more involved when making changes to it. After all, it is a software program. Then once it is changed it needs to be pushed out to those people who have already downloaded it for them to download again. Also to consider is that each version, be it for Apple or Android, needs to be updated, adding to the complexity required to maintain them.

Search Engine Friendly
Mobile websites can be searched for, and found easily using any search engine desired.

When searching in a smartphone most people will likely search on Google. That means they will be finding websites, not mobile apps. People don't go to an app marketplace looking for where to eat or shop. They use a search engine to look for websites.

Most smart phones have a search engine like Google already installed when they are purchased. And the volume of searches occurring on mobile devices is growing at an astonishing rate.

It is also important to note that with the proper redirection code installed on your standard desktop/laptop website, a mobile searcher will automatically be redirected to your mobile website.

Contrast this visibility to that of an app, where they are only found in an app marketplace.

Easy to Share
Just like any other website URL, it is very easy for some one to share the URL of a mobile site. Emails, text messages, Facebook, Twitter, or any other means of communication can be utilized.

In fact, with the proper redirection code installed on your standard website, mobile users don't even need to know the mobile URL. They just go to your standard site, and they are automatically redirected to the mobile site.

Additionally, it doesn't matter which platform, Apple or Android, some one is using, because mobile websites are platform independent.

This is much simpler and easier than trying to share a mobile app, which is of course, platform dependent.

Longevity

A mobile website cannot be deleted from a user's phone. Because it's not on their phone, it's on the internet. Its out there for as long as you want it to be. Always available for people to return to.

Apps on the other hand have a much shorter lifespan. A user may grow tired of it, loose interest, or just not need it anymore, and then deletes the app from their phone.

Cheaper and Quicker to Publish

Mobile websites are generally quicker and less expensive to publish online. A mobile app will cost considerably more, and take significantly longer to get to market. And, if you want every-one to have access to it, you need at least two different versions. Again, a mobile app is NOT platform independent like a mobile website is.

Support and Maintenance
The investment in both a mobile website and a mobile app doesn't end with the initial publication. Changing an app requires programming. It will have to be re-approved by the app marketplace, and it's entirely possible that with changes to hardware and smartphone operating systems you'll need to change the mobile app as well.

Over time properly supporting, maintaining, and upgrading the mobile app is much more expensive and complex than for a mobile website.

When is an Mobile App Appropriate?

Even though there are many inherent benefits of having a mobile website, there are still times that a mobile app would be more appropriate. Generally speaking, if your needs fall into one of the following scenarios then an app should be seriously considered.

- **Interaction & Gaming** – For interactive gaming an app is almost always going to be a better choice that a mobile website.

- **Personalization** – If your target audience needs to customize or personalize what they need to do on a regular basis, the app is a better application for this.

- **Calculations & Reporting** – When it comes to crunching numbers and data manipulation, both of which require a fair bit of power, then an app would be better suited to that.

- **Processing Power** – If you need more processing power than what a browser can provide then an app can handle that better than a website.

- **No internet connection required** – (Except to download the app.) If you need to provide offline functions without the access to the internet either by 3G or wireless connectivity, then apps are what you need to do that.

The bottom line.

So, which is better? Or, perhaps it's better asked, which is better for you? That all depends on why you want to go mobile.

If your goal is to provide an application that needs to work more like a computer program, but on a mobile device, then the mobile app is the way to go.

However, if your primary goal for going mobile is marketing driven, and you want more exposure to those who use their mobile devices, then you need to ask yourself this question.

If some one is looking for information about what I sell – my products and/or services, my location, my menu, my catalog, my hours, or anything else I want them to know about me, where will they search – in an app marketplace, or on the internet?

Mobile Website Examples

With all this talk about mobile websites, it's probably time for some examples. This will allow you to see the major differences between a desktop/laptop website, and one that is designed for mobile devices.

You will notice a couple of major themes here.

One, absolutely no horizontal scrolling. People on smartphones truly hate this. So these mobile sites completely eliminate that.

Two, minimal vertical scrolling. The home page of each site is very compact, so that the visitor gets the gist of what the website is all about very quickly.

Three, no need for zooming in and out just to be able to read the content. The font style, and font size enable some one to read the site without this aggravating zooming in and out.

Four, intuitive navigation. These sites are easy to figure out how to navigate away from the home page to get to the information people are looking for.

Five, in spite of the fact that they appear in this book as black and white, mobile websites can be made to be quite attractive.

Example 1.

As you can see, the title and the phone number are useful here, but that is all.

The logo is missing, the are only two navigation icons appearing, and the page's text is only three characters wide. Not very inviting for the visitor.

Here is the mobile version for example 1.

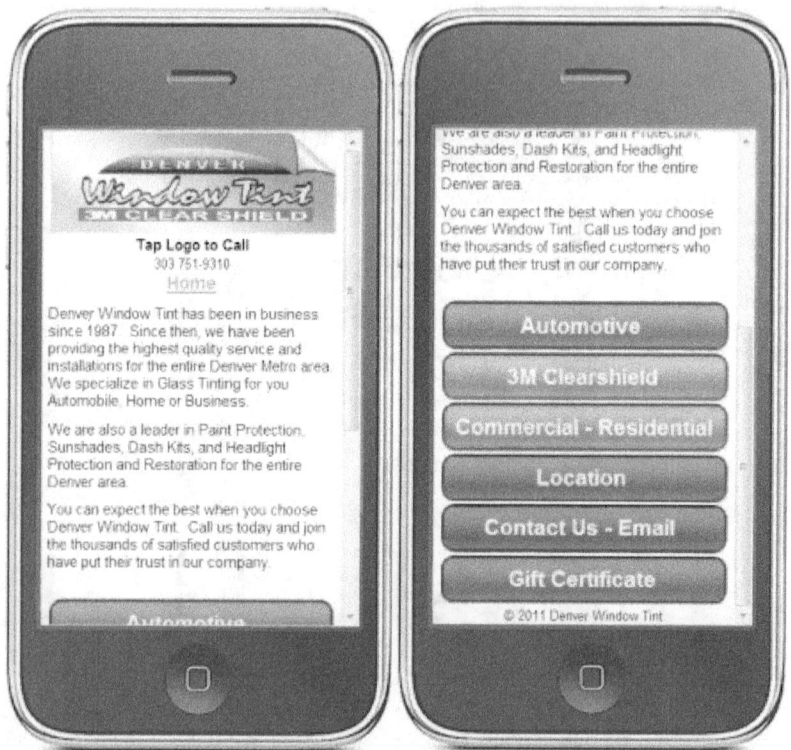

The logo is visible. The logo has a 'Tap to Call' feature, where if the visitor taps the logo, the phone application instantly pops up with the number already inserted, enabling one-touch calling.

The text is readable, there is no horizontal scrolling required, also no zooming required. With only minimal vertical scrolling the navigation buttons are visible and intuitive.

Example 2.

As you can see, the title is visible. The menu bars are visible, but are to small for adult fingers to reliably use. And there is no contact information showing.

Also, only a sliver of the home page photo is visible.

Here is the mobile version for example 2.

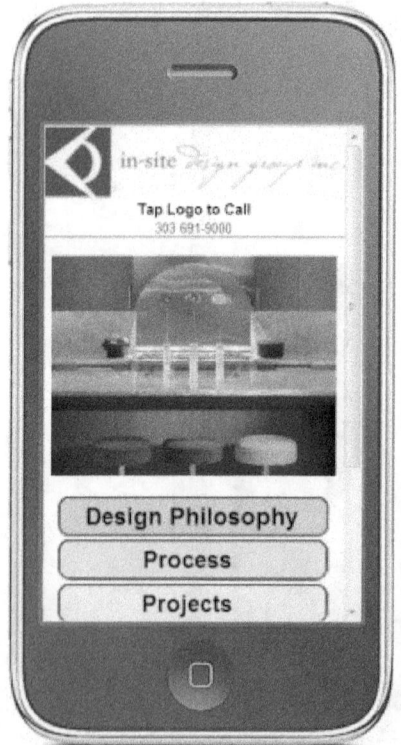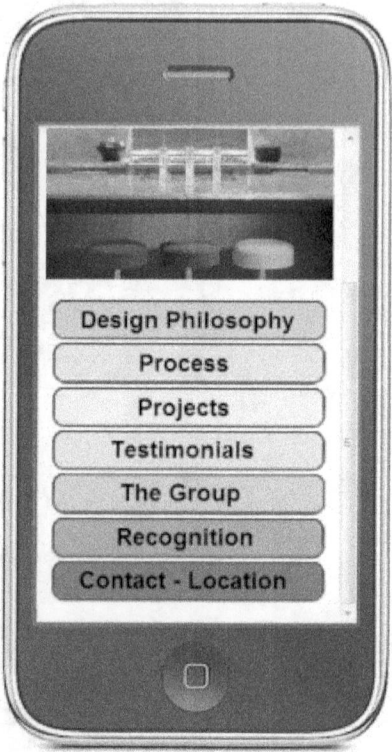

Here we have a complete home page photo, and the logo has the 'Tap to Call' feature. Again there is no horizontal scrolling, and no zooming in and out. And with minimal vertical scrolling, the navigation buttons are visible, intuitive, and sized for adult fingers.

Example 3.

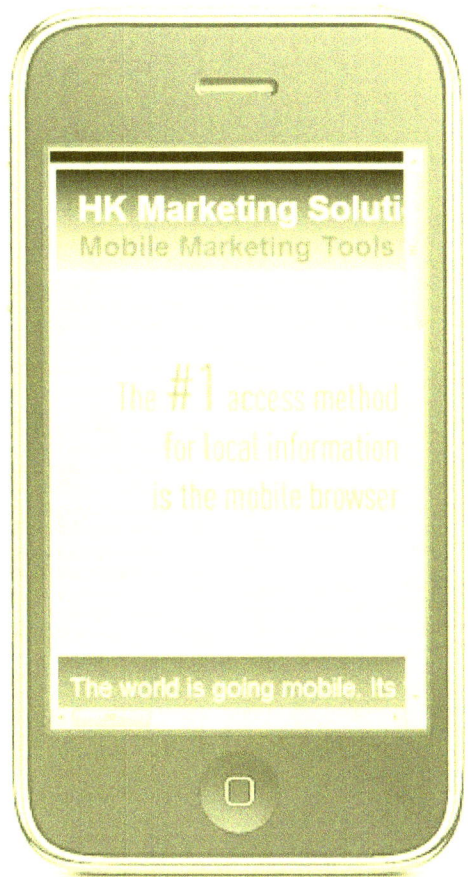

Here you can see that the title and header are not completely visible, and horizontal scrolling is required just to see what this site is all about.

There is no navigation means available, and very little other information showing without large-scale scrolling and zooming.

Here is the mobile version for example 3.

Now we can see the title and header just fine, and the phone number is highly visible. The text is readable without scrolling and zooming. And the navigation is sized appropriately and is intuitive. Very easy to use. There is also a link back to the home page, and a 'Tap to Call' feature located in the footer of each page.

Example 4.

With this site the logo is too small, and difficult to read. Most of the navigation is not visible without horizontal scrolling, as is the text, and there is no quick way to see contact and location informa-tion.

Here is the mobile version for example 4.

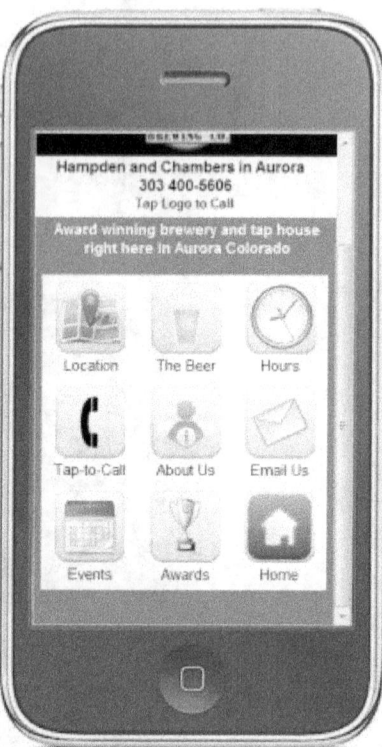

Now you can see the logo is larger and easier to read. The location and phone number are at the top and prominent. And the logo has the 'Tap to Call' feature.

Also, by using icons instead of vertical menu buttons, it gives the site an 'Apple' look and feel. Very intuitive and easy to navigate.

The Pros and Cons of Mobile Marketing

Like any dynamic new technology, mobile marketing contains advantages and disadvantages to the business owner new to this type of marketing. In this chapter I will lay out some of the pros and cons of this technology, so that you can create an informed opinion for yourself whether mobile marketing is a good fit for your own business.

First of all, to the "uninitiated", managing your mobile marketing campaigns correctly and effectively can prove to be quite challenging. There are just so many different variables that can contribute to a bad campaign, as well as to a good campaign.

Local mobile search advertising and marketing is not as established as local desktop search marketing is. Although it is estimated that advertisers and marketers are going to spend $11.5 billion globally on mobile marketing this year.

The actual number of cellular phone users is also expected to advance to over 5 billion this year. In the United States alone, there are over 300 million cell phone subscribers. The number is expected to double within the next few years.

This makes mobile marketing and advertising the next big thing in the marketing community. We seem to be on the edge of a whole new era in mobile technology. However, there are quite a few challenges to be dealt with by the business owner who is new to mobile marketing. Let's have a look at both the advantages and disadvantages of this technology.

Pros:

- There is high coverage of cell phone devices with at least as many mobile users as PC users.

- Internet searches on cell phones will soon exceed searches done on personal computers.

- Mobile technology provides access to many buyers who cannot afford personal computers.

- Cell phones are able to receive input at anytime from anywhere. This enables advertising designed for specific locations. It also enables marketing campaigns that are based on buying behavior.

- Mobile phones are very personal devices that individuals tend to take wherever they go. This makes it very convenient for advertisers to create and nurture a relationship with their target market.

- Mobile technology provides new ways for advertisers and marketers to communicate with target markets.

- Cell phone marketing programs can be specialized and targeted. This makes them more successful than traditional forms of marketing.

- Cell phone SMS text message marketing campaigns are opt-in enabled. This means that the people receiving the advertisements have already shown an interest in the services and products offered.

- Cell phone SMS text message marketing can also assist in building a customer list. Once the individuals have opted to receive marketing and advertisements from your company, you are able to use the information to promote your business further.

- Mobile advertising can help to create a buzz about your company, services, and products. Due to the fact that your marketing messages will reach their intended audience while they are socializing, shopping and making purchase decisions, you can experience a much higher response rate.

Cons:

- Some consumers have a general distrust of receiving marketing messages on their cell phone, and consider it a form of "spam". However, they did elect to sign up. And they can cancel at any time. So this isn't a big deal.

- There is a huge scarcity of sites that are mobile ready at this moment. (Only eight percent of the top one thousand U.S. brands have a mobile website)

- There is a period of trial and error required for

those who use mobile advertising and marketing. It is different than the usual web marketing.

- Penetration of devices with 3G is also very low in many countries around the globe. However, North America has wide 3G coverage.

There are many more things to know and understand about mobile marketing methods besides the above listed points. Ideally you want to know what methods work the best, how to effectively segment and target your buyers, and then combine everything into a successful campaign. That's what this book is all about.

Introduction to Text Message Marketing

Recent developments in technology have done much to change our lives. Each day, new ideas are turned into objects that are meant to make our lives easier. As new technologies continue to develop, businesses are forced to keep up if they want to grow and prosper in today's tough economic environment.

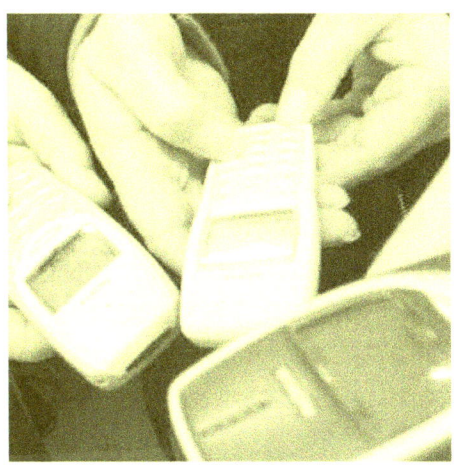

Today's most advanced means of communication revolves around mobile phones. Mobile communications continue to improve as more features and functionalities are added. In fact, some smart phones are better equipped than desktop computers!

For these reasons, businesses need to start "mobilizing" if they want to really stay in front of their target market.

The most popular form of mobile marketing is SMS Text Message Marketing. What is SMS? It stands for "short message service", and it gives you the ability to communicate directly to your target market by sending a simple, quick text message. This permission-based method is perfect because your recipients have opted-in to receive your messages. The best part is that it's effective because they WANT to receive your messages

SMS text messaging is all about the deliverability of the message. Most are read within minutes of be received. In fact, recent studies show that 97% of text messages are read within minutes of receiving them making this is the perfect way to get your message across to your target market.

A benefit of SMS text massaging is that its more time-efficient compared to traditional advertising methods. There are character limits on messages so they have to be short, so putting together your marketing message takes just a few minutes instead of much longer to prepare.

Also, you can obtain metrics on the status of your messages as well. You have the advantage of monitoring and finding out what happens with each message you send out since it's traceable.

SMS text messaging is a low cost means of re-taining customers. These are customers who have already spent money with you, so chances are, they will come back to spend more money with you as long as you keep in touch with them.

There are many different marketing strategies available today for business owners but not all of them are as effective and profitable as a SMS text message marketing campaign. If everything is set-up well and you are taking good care of your list, your business can bring in a lot more money with the use of this amazingly effective technology.

Mobile Text Messaging Guidelines

Every day millions of Americans use their mobile phones to communicate with each other. In fact, text messaging is becoming more common than phone calls via their mobile devices.

From a business perspective, mobile phones are one of the most essential devices and a necessity to most people. In light of that, marketing strategies using mobile promotions are being utilized by many businesses to reach out to potential customers – including SMS text message marketing.

For SMS text marketing to be effective, proper planning and execution is essential in order to get the best return on your investment (ROI). How you communicate through SMS text marketing has a big impact on the outcome of your goals.

Here are a few guidelines for all of your text messages:

1. Limited space.

Make sure that your text message is suc-
cinct and to the point. Ideally try to keep it
at a maximum length of 160 characters, as
this is the limit for most text messages.

2. Your business name.

This sounds like common sense; however,
you would be surprised how many small
business owners forget to even include the
name of their business in every text message.

The name of your business lets you brand
yourself and your company, and makes all
of your messages identifiable to the end
user. People want to know exactly who
they are receiving messages from. This
will put them at ease as they know exactly
why they are receiving the message and
hopefully make them a repeat customer.

You can do this by listing your company's
name as the "sender", and also by including the name of your business in the body
of the message itself.

3. Be friendly.

Be polite, friendly, and respectful. These are people you want to spend money with you. Treat them that way.

4. Free stuff is always good.

Providing free information is a great way to find a receptive audience to your text messages. Giving away free information, coupons, rebates, and similar promotions will always increase customer loyalty and keep them coming back for more.

5. Always give them the option to opt-out.

SMS Text Message marketing allows people to opt-in to your list, which means they WANT to receive your promotional offers and messages. However, there should be an easy way to opt-out of the list if someone really wants to do so. This option to opt-out makes a lot of people feel more at ease when the time comes for opting-in to your list.

6. Include a "Call-to-Action"

Be sure to TELL people what you want them to do. If you don't tell them exactly what to do, you will rarely get the results that you want. For instance, if you want them to bring the coupon for a free pizza into your restaurant, tell them exactly how to do that.

Utilizing Mobile Coupons to Promote Your Business

Okay, here's a fact of human nature: people love "freebies", and the idea of getting something for nothing is irresistible to consumers. This idea can be easily incorporated into your mobile marketing campaign by offering discounts and coupons that customers can access directly from their mobile devices.

However, don't just offer freebies or discounts randomly; rather, a considered and systematic approach is necessary in order to achieve the best results.

Think very carefully about what services you can afford to offer at a discount (or not charge for at all), while at the same time keeping in mind what your customers want and need the most. And what they perceive to have high value.

In some cases, useless freebies may actually cheapen your business image, and can even offend your market. A really great way to use coupons is to gather a list of previous customers who have spent money on your products and services. Sending them coupons or discounts on future purchases can add to customer loyalty.

Most people with mobile phones tend to keep them within arm's reach virtually all the time. They tend to carry them to work, to play, shopping, running errands, almost everywhere they go. Therefore, your SMS coupons are likely to be read by consumers just minutes after your send them out.

Once they receive an SMS with a coupon, they are much more likely to open it. The chances of a response or an action are also greatly increased.

What does "mobile marketing coupons" really refer to? It is one effective way of reaching out and connecting with your target market by means of a "tried and true" method – the coupon. Your promotion will be received fast without having to scan papers and wait for monthly magazine issues. Unlike the traditional paper coupons, mobile coupons are not easy to lose.

Imagine getting an SMS with a coupon to your favorite store. Let's say you're a musician and you play the bass guitar. Guitar Center has just sent you a coupon for 30% off all bass strings.

You see the coupon and the next day you make your purchase with the discount.

These coupons can be used instantly, right there from the phone by presenting the coupon at your business. In addition, SMS text coupons are more unique and compelling, and will therefore convert much better than printed coupons.

In fact, SMS coupons have been shown to out-perform standard printed coupons by a vast mar-gin. There is also the viral nature of a "virtual" coupon, as they can be instantly shared among a prospect's friends and family. Mobile coupons are more talked about and more easily shared than printed coupons.

The concept of mobile marketing coupons is the best way to capitalize on the local mobile market for your business. It helps increase profits be-cause you are marketing your products and ser-vices to a list of customers that WANT your pro-motions. Mobile coupons are the perfect way to keep your list active and excited to be a part of your SMS text message marketing list.

Text Marketing Mistakes That Can Damage Your Business

Mobile marketing is one of the most cost-effective online promotional strategies for one simple reason: because it gives businesses the ability to reach a targeted audience wherever they are.

They no longer need to be tethered to a home-based computer in order to receive information. Billions of people use mobile devices every day, so the correct mobile marketing strategy will allow your business to capitalize on this enormous potential customer base. Unfortunately, many businesses today are NOT utilizing the full capability that mobile marketing offers to increase profits and ROI – Return On Investment.

Are you looking for a way to build a massive list of loyal customers that are seeking out your products and services over and over? Then here are a few SMS text message marketing mistakes you need to be aware of and avoid.

Not Including a "Call to Action"

If your text messaging does not contain a call to action then you are really missing the boat. What is a call to action? It can be as simple as saying "Show this message to receive your discount".   If you don't tell your prospects exactly what you would like them to do, chances are they won't take any action at all, and a valuable opportunity to have them opt-in to your list, or discover more information about your products or services is squandered

No "Carrot" For Signing Up

Everyone loves a bonus. So an effective marketing strategy is to offer your potential customers a valuable sign-up bonus as incentive to join your list. This can be an instant reward like a coupon. For example, you might send a text message that says "Show this text message to Fancy Pizza today for 10% off your order". Or "Show this text message to receive 10% off your next purchase."

Spamming Your Subscribers

Many customers love getting text messages like the one above, but hate feeling like they are being spammed. You must be mindful to scale your periodic texts to an acceptable rate. Too many might force the user to opt-out of your list forever, which is certainly counter-productive to your mobile marketing campaign. Text messages sent a few times per month will keep the customer anticipating your next special deal, and keep their interest high in your marketing campaign.

No "Thank-You" Incentives

Because you want to keep current customers happy and wanting more, you don't want every message that you send to them overtly be a promotional in nature. An effective way to accomplish this is to offer "freebies" to your subscribers every now and then. These can be simple like sending a text message that says "FREE STUFF - 2 days only!" or "1/2 off all purchased items". Your list needs some exciting offers to keep it fresh.

No Strategy for Referrals

It's important to tap into the viral nature of text messaging. To do this you will want to have your customers sharing information about you and your business with their friends and family. Therefore your offers of products and services should have a "Refer a Friend" component to them. Give your "referring" customers a nice reward for referring others and watch your list (and your bottom line) quickly grow. A satisfied customer will very likely refer your site to a friend if you give them an opportunity.

QR Codes Explained

Today, large companies are incorporating the exciting new technology of QR codes in their overall marketing strategy, and they are a perfect fit for mobile marketing.

"QR codes" stands for Quick Response codes which were originally created by Japanese car manufacturers for the purpose of tracking car parts during the assembly process. Today, they are gaining popularity all over the world because they offer consumers the ability to quickly scan information and data with mobile devices.

These QR codes are distinctive, consisting of specially patterned black squares against a white background. Data is embedded with these codes and accessed via a click with a mobile phone camera. Business can utilize QR codes to

support product discounts, special offers, to promote new coupons, provide additional product information and manuals, or to send them to your
web page, Facebook fan page, or any other web
property.

Here are some advantage to using the power of
QR codes in your own business:

1. No Printing Costs

One benefit of QR codes is that you do not
need to reprint advertisements or flyers
every time you change a particular promotion. Simply clicking to QR code will trigger
the mobile phone to go to the source and
download the most current information
about that product. Your customers can
therefore click this exact same code anytime and get the most up to date information.

2. Enhance Customer Communications

Adding QR codes to your product line will
add a new layer of excitement for the customer. They will want to scan your image
to see if anything has changed since the
last time they clicked your image. This in-

formation will appear instantly and provide instant gratification for your customer.

3. Fast Response

The best thing about these "quick" codes is that they represent instant delivery of information wherever the code is scanned. This means that the consumer no longer has to wait to get home, turn on their desktop computer, etc. in order to research your product or service. At the end of the day, QR codes facilitate immediate access to information about your business, products, and services, which make them an invaluable addition to your mobile marketing campaign.

QR codes can also be used to conduct surveys and obtain customer feedback about your product or service. And even though QR codes are still fairly new, consumers already recognize and are using them in magazines, websites, brochures, and even in retail stores.

Using QR Codes in Your Business

So just what can a "QR Code" do for your business? Below are several examples of how you can immediately incorporate QR codes into your current marketing strategy.

1. Social Platforms

With the popularity of social media, QR codes can be added to your business web pages or social media profiles such as Facebook. This will give potential customers the ability to instantly scan your codes and connect to the information they are seeking.

2. Business Cards

Another means of using QR codes effectively is adding the code to your business card so the customer can connect directly to your company's website, Fanpage, or any other online promotion that you wish.

3. Product Packaging

If you deliver packages to your customers, QR code can be used to direct them to on-line manuals or presentations on how to use that product. A simple but effective strategy that can be easily implemented with a sticker applied to the package.

4. Electronic Press Releases

The power of an online press release can be multiplied by incorporating the inclusion of a QR code. Once you have the cus-tomer's attention and wanting more, they will notice the QR code at the bottom of the page and click that image. Then you can take them to a larger article or a web page that promotes that product or service you just described.

5. All Printed Promotional Material

Branding your business and products can be greatly enhanced via QR codes, and many businesses are adding them to all printed promotional materials and advert-isements. In fact, you may have already noticed them yourself on postcards, bill-boards, magazine ads and in newspapers.

This strategy allows businesses to easily target your customers with specific informa-tion that will keep them coming back for more.

Here are some more ideas to get you thinking about this.

o **On For Sale signs.** Whether residential or commercial, for sale signs could include codes that had all the information a sell sheet includes, plus video and photo walk-throughs.

o **Next to packaged food in groceries.** Give shoppers quick access to recipes that in-clude the ingredients they see on the shelf.

o **On bottles of wine.** It would be nice to be able to get info about the vineyard, and maybe buy a case of that bottle just en-joyed at the restaurant.

o **For conference signage.** Next to the name of the upcoming sessions in each room would be the QR code so you could get the full description, outlines, speaker bios, and other additional information.

- **On liquor bottles.** Linked to drink recipes; this would be especially good for new drinks you're bringing to market.

- **On the safety bar ads on ski mountain chair lifts.** These days, everyone on the mountain seems to have a smart phone, and they're going to be a captive audience for 5 – 10 minutes, sitting on that chair going up the mountain.

- **Inside elevators.** Advertisements inside elevators for products and/or services that cater to downtown business people. Such as dry cleaning, flowers, or lunch catering.

- **On coffee cups from your local coffee shop.** Plenty of advertising opportunities here.

- **On trade show booths.** Scan a picture, (be entered to) win something.

- **On recipes in magazines.** Quick link to videos, reviews and feedback at the website.

- **Posted on car windows in dealerships.** Perfect for after-hour shoppers.

o **On movie posters.** QR code takes them to a preview of the movie.

o **Business cards.** The back side.

Mobile Marketing's Return on Investment

When deciding on a marketing plan it goes without saying that if you aren't measuring, then you're just guessing. If you don't know at the start what your expected results are, and what your costs are to attain those results, then you're just throwing money against the wall to see what sticks.

If you have an unlimited marketing budget then that's probably alright. But in this current economic environment, that's probably not your situation.

That's where ROI, return on investment, comes in.

At first glance it may appear that quantifying mobile marketing ROI is a daunting task. The term seems to be rather broad, at least in the minds of many business owners who haven't yet studied it.

What exactly makes up mobile marketing? What kind of metrics can we use to measure it's effectiveness? How will I know if its worth jumping into?

We've already defined the three main pieces of mobile marketing – Mobile Website, SMS Text Marketing, and QR Codes. Now we have to see if there is a way to measure their effectiveness.

It may already be obvious that one of these is going to be easier to quantify than the other two. SMS text marketing will be the easiest to measure. The other two address communication, customer experience, building relationships, and providing alternate means for potential customers to find you, learn more about you and your products, and then buy from you.

Here we will break down the three main avenues of mobile marketing and see if, and how, we can measure their effectiveness.

Mobile website ROI.

How does one quantify an enhanced customer experience? Can you put a dollar value on a more 'friendly' site? How can you tell if having a simpler, easier to use, and more intuitive mobile site is positively effecting your bottom line?

All good questions. And all without easily dis-
cernible answers. However, there is a tool that
will give us some valid indications as to the success or failure of a mobile website; it's called
Google Analytics.

Google analytics is a snippet of code that is inserted into the mobile website that will allow
Google to accumulate statistics about how visitors are interacting with the website. (In fact,
Google analytics should be used on all websites
regardless of whether they are designed for mobile devices, or desktop/laptop computers.)

The list of statistics gathered and made available
is extensive, and include:
    Number of visitors.
    How long they stayed on the site.
    How many pages they viewed while on your
    site.
    Percentage of first time, or repeat visitors.
    How they found your site.
    What search terms were used to find your
    site.
    How many visited using a mobile device.

If you want to know how your website (mobile or
desktop/laptop) is performing, then this kind of information is quite valuable.

How many visitors will tell you if your site is properly optimized for the search engines. What search terms used to find your site will also tell you something about optimization.

How long visitors stayed on your site, and how many different pages they viewed tells you something about your content and how easy and intuitive your navigation is.

Percentage of first time visitors also says something about your optimization, and percentage of repeat visitors tells you whether or not visitors find your site useful and valuable.

Can you put a dollar amount on this information and statistics? Probably not, at least not in a way that you could plug into a spreadsheet. Will your business see a boost from a more effective and efficient website, (mobile and desktop/laptop), that engages your visitors and gives they what they are looking for? Certainly yes.

SMS Text Marketing ROI.

This is the easiest of the mobile marketing techniques to quantify and put a dollar value on. Even in a 'spreadsheet' kind of way. That is because it's relatively easy to determine additional costs, and additional revenues.

Let's run through a simple analysis to make measuring a bit easier.

A restaurant starts a text marketing campaign.

4 new customers sign up for text messaging per day, enticed by an instant coupon.

The instant coupon is for a free drink with each entrée ordered.

Cost = $1 per instant coupon, (the free drink).

After 3 months, that's 360 customers in the data-base, and $360 in costs.

4 text messaging blasts go out in the fourth month with a special offer coupon.

4 blasts x 360 mobile phone numbers in data-base = 1440 text messages sent out.

4% coupon redemption rate (very conservative) = 57 coupons returned by returning customers.

$30 average bill per table.

57 coupons x $30 = $1,710 in increased reven-ue.

Cost of coupon @ $2.50 x 57 coupons redeemed = $142.50

Cost of text messages @ $0.10 each x 1440 = $144.00

Increase in revenue = $1,710
Cost of enticement instant coupons = $360.00
Cost of text message coupons = $142.50
Cost of sending the messages = $144.00
Total costs = $646.50
Net (New revenues – new costs) = $1,063.50
Return on investment = 61%

Now let's convert this into a scenario.

Mike is the owner of a sports bar/restaurant called Mike's Place. He decides to use text messaging in order to increase his repeat business, enhance his customer loyalty and raise his long-term customer value.

On each table he displays a table tent inviting his guests to text 'freedrink' to 75757. When they do, his guests receive an instant return text message which they then show their server in order to receive a free drink for each entrée they order. This also enrolls the customers into Mike's database of mobile phone numbers.

This happens about four times per day. So that after 3 months Mike has a database of about 360 mobile phone numbers.

Mike decides to run four specials each month for which he will send out text messages coupons.

One for a 'Monday Night Football' special of a free beer with each entrée when purchased on Monday evenings from 6pm till 11pm. This message will be sent out on a Monday mid-afternoon.

Another special for just Saturday from noon till 6pm called the 'College Football Special'. This is for a free order of chicken wings with each pitcher of beer ordered. This text will be sent out Saturday morning.

Another special is called the 'Midweek Special' and is for Tuesdays and Wednesdays evening only. Free soup or salad with any entrée. These are usually his slowest evenings. This text is sent out on a Tuesday afternoon.

The last monthly special is a lunch special for any weekday from 11am till 3pm for a free bowel of soup with any salad entrée purchased. This is sent out mid-morning on a Monday.

All the customer has to do in order to receive their savings is to show the text message coupon that they received on their phone to their server.

Of course each of these text messages could be sent out each week, but for this example we'll keep it simple.

So in a months time there are a total of 1,440 texts sent out to the 360 mobile phone numbers in Mike's database of customer mobile phone numbers.

Out of these 1,440 text messages about 4%, or 57 of the text coupons are redeemed. (This is conservative.)

If the average bill per table is about $30, then that's in increase in revenues of $1,710.

So now we figure the costs. $1 per enticement instant coupon x 360 people = $360.

Average cost per text message coupon of $2.50 x 57 coupons = $142.50.

Cost of text messages at $0.10 per message x 1,440 messages = $144.00

Altogether the numbers look like this:

Increase in Revenue	1,710.00
Enticement Coupon Costs	360.00
Text Message Coupon Costs	142.50
Text Messaging Costs	144.00
Total Costs	646.50
Net (new revenues – new costs)	**1,063.50**
Return on Investment	**61%**

As you can see Mike has returned a tidy sum for his investment.

These specials can be most anything you dream up. And of course, can be tailored to your individual business.

QR Codes ROI.

QR codes are rarely a stand-alone marketing technique. They are used primarily to boost or enhance another form of marketing, most often printed pieces.

They can also be looked at as a gateway. A gateway to provide more information, to more customer interaction, to an enhanced customer experience, and to increased return on investment for the other marketing efforts that the QR code is partnered with.

Besides boosting other methods of marketing, QR codes greatly enhance your ability to track and measure the effectiveness of whatever other marketing efforts they are coupled with.

To see how to measure their effects lets look at a very basic example.

You've placed a print ad in the local paper or local magazine. You have your usual visuals and copy. And lets say you direct them to your website for more information and some special offers.

Someone sees your ad. Where are they when they do? Do they run to their computer to check out your website? Are they anywhere near their computer? Will they remember your website's address when they finally get to a computer? Will they even remember your business name so they can search for it later?

These are difficult questions to answer.

Now suppose you had inserted a QR code on that print ad. And when scanned, the QR code takes the reader directly to your mobile website. And like nearly everyone else, their smartphone is within arm's reach.

Now, it's a very simple matter for them to get to your mobile website almost immediately. They scan the code, and they are there. The increased convenience is phenomenal. The increased traffic to your mobile website is <u>measurable</u>. And the person interested in what you are offering has immediate gratification.

Your return on investment for that print ad has just been improved

Or suppose that the QR code takes the reader to an online coupon. They scan the code, see the online coupon on their phone, save it as a bookmark, present it at the time of purchase just like a printed coupon, and suddenly your coupon redemption rate skyrockets.

You can track how many people visited that online coupon, and how many people redeemed the coupon. Would this kind of information help you craft better, more effective offers? Probably.

There are two important things to note here.

First, is that the QR code takes the user to an online location. And with the proper reporting tools in place you can track and measure the traffic to that location.

Second, the QR code has actually made that print ad more effective by allowing the reader to take instant action, and do so with ease.

Glossary

Acquisition rate – The total number of participants who were offered to opt in on a mobile marketing campaign divided by the total audience. The percent gives you the number of respondents who opt in.

Alerts – Notifications, typically in the form of a text message, containing time-sensitive information (event details, company updates, coupons, special offers) that are pushed to a mobile subscriber who has opted-in to receive this information.

Analytics – Your text message marketing vendor should provide you with some kind of reporting system that will give you an idea of how your texts are being sent, opened, how many unsubscribes etc… These tools are sometimes known as Analytics or Metrics.

Blast – A blast is when you send a message to everyone on your list. This can be an update or an offer designed to get people in the door.

Call-to-Action (CTA) – This is an instruction to the reader to act on the message that was received. The action could be to click a link, send a mobile text, visit a website, call a phone number, or other types of actions.

Characters – When text messaging, this term means all of the numbers, letters, symbols and spaces of a text message. Anything you input is a character and most text messages are limited to around 160.

Click to Call – A link on a mobile website that when clicked, instantly initiates a call from that phone to a pre-specified number.

Click-through Rate (CTR) – this is a common measurement used to determine the number of users who clicked to access more information or take action resulting from a mobile marketing campaign message.

Flash – Is streaming animation for web pages. Sometimes Flash is a portion of an HTML web page, and sometimes a web page is made entirely of Flash. Either way, Flash files are called "Flash movies". Flash does not play well on mobile websites, and should be avoided.

Keyword – In text message marketing this is the term that people will text to a certain number to join your list. For example, you may see an ad that says: "Text the word PIZZAJOE to 72727." The word "PIZZAJOE" is the keyword.

Message Based Pricing – This is a pricing model in which you will be charged per message you send. It usually works out to pennies a message.

Mobile Search – Executing a search via mobile Internet.

Mobile Site – A website that is made specifically to display well on mobile devices. Also known as a mobile-friendly or mobile-ready website.

Opt-In – In text message marketing, this term means that someone has willingly added themselves to "Your List". This is usually done by texting a keyword, to a short code number.

Opt-In Offer – This is the offer that you use to entice people to opt-in to your list. For most business this will be some sort of freebie, coupon or discount.

Permission Based – Permission based marketing is based around the general concept that you first get people to give you permission to market to them through the opt-in process. This increases your return on investment, and customer satisfaction.

QR Code – A QR code (abbreviated from Quick Response code) is a specific matrix barcode (or two-dimensional code) that is readable by smart-phones . The code consists of black modules arranged in a square pattern on a white background. The information encoded may be text, a URL, or other data.

Short Message Service (SMS) – SMS is a service available on most digital mobile phones that permits the sending of short messages (160 characters) between mobile phones and other handheld devices. SMS is commonly referred to as simply text messaging

SMTP – Simple Mail Transfer Protocol (SMTP) is an Internet standard for electronic mail (e-mail) transmission. This is a much slower and less reliable way to send text messages. Inferior providers use this form of messaging. It is cheaper, so the appearance of value is there, but the deliverability is not.

SMPP – The Short Message Peer-to-Peer (SMPP) protocol is a telecommunications industry protocol for exchanging text messages between yourself and your list. This is a much more effective choice when text message marketing.

Short Code – Short codes (also known as short numbers) are special telephone numbers, significantly shorter than full telephone numbers, that are used for text message marketing campaigns. This will be the number that people text the keyword to.

Tap to Call – A feature that allows a smartphone user to 'tap' a certain area of their screen when viewing a mobile website, and automatically initiate a phone call to the website's owner.

Your List – This is your list of people who have opted-in. In text message marketing this will be a list of mobile phone numbers from the people who have joined your list. This is who you now can directly market to.

About the Author

Consultant, author, and online marketing professional Loren Squires is an expert at helping small businesses and entrepreneurs gain a competitive advantage in their local marketplace.

He makes sure that these businesses are able to be "found" on the internet, ensures that they never run out of leads, and helps them to transform these potential clients into lifetime customers (and raving fans!).

If you are serious about improving your own business' bottom line, and would like to schedule a free consultation to see how Loren can create a comprehensive online marketing campaign for your company, you can contact him at 303 280-3451. Or by sending an email to LorenSquires@gmail.com.

For additional mobile marketing information visit: Moblie-Marketing-Colorado.com